RACLETTE

© Neuer Pawlak Verlag, a subsidiary of
VEMAG Verlags- und Medien Aktiengesellschaft, Cologne
www.apollo-intermedia.de

Picture credits: Neuer Pawlak Verlag, Cologne
Complete production: VEMAG Verlags- und Medien Aktiengesellschaft, Cologne
Printed in Germany

RACLETTE

CONTENTS

Raclette Snacks –
A light meal
with a difference

MUSHROOM RACLETTE

FOR 4 SERVINGS:

250 g/9 oz large fresh mushrooms
½ bunch of parsley
100 g/3½ oz double cream cheese
Salt
Freshly ground pepper
150 g/5 oz grated Gouda cheese
Herbs, to garnish

1. Trim and wash the mushrooms and cut the stalks off.
2. Wash the parsley, shake dry and chop up finely. Stir into the cream cheese and season with salt and pepper.
3. Fill the mushrooms with the cream cheese, place in the raclette pans and sprinkle the cheese on top.
4. Gratinate everything under the raclette for approx. 8 minutes. Serve garnished with the herbs.

Per serving: approx. 812 kj/193 kcal, 14 g P, 12 g F, 2 g C

ITALIAN RACLETTE

FOR 4 SERVINGS:

8 baguette slices
1 honey melon (300 g/10½ oz)
100 g/3½ oz Parma ham
150 g/5 oz Parmesan cheese
Herbs, to garnish

1. Toast the baguette slices. Slice the honey melon in half, remove the pips and use a fruit scoop or a teaspoon to make small ball shapes. Slice the ham thinly. Grate the cheese.
2. Place one baguette slice into each raclette pan. Top with the ham slices and cover these with the melon balls.
3. Sprinkle with the grated cheese and gratinate under the raclette grill for approx. 8 minutes. Serve garnished with the herbs.

Per serving: approx. 909 kj/216 kcal, 13 g P, 9 g F, 15 g C

AMERICAN RACLETTE

FOR 4 SERVINGS:

8 corn cobs (preserved;
480 g/1 lb drained weight)

2 cloves of garlic

1 chilli pepper

1 bunch of parsley

3 tbsp oil

Salt

Freshly ground pepper

1 red sweet bell pepper

150 g/5 oz smoked cheese
with ham pieces

1. Drain the corn cobs. Peel the garlic cloves and press them out. Trim, wash and cut the chilli pepper in half, remove the seeds and then chop up finely.
2. Wash the parsley, shake dry and chop up finely. Combine the oil, garlic, chilli pepper and parsley and stir together. Season with the salt and pepper.
3. Brush the corn cobs with the oil mixture and grill for approx. 8 minutes. Repeatedly brush with the oil.
4. Cut the corn cobs into slices. Trim, wash and half the sweet

bell pepper then remove the seeds and the white flesh. Cut the pepper into strips.
5. Place some pepper strips and corn slices into each raclette pan. Grate the cheese and sprinkle over the top. Gratinate everything under the raclette grill for approx. 6 minutes. Slices of toast go very well with this.

Per serving: approx. 1 752 kj/417 kcal,
13 g P, 17 g F, 46 g C

Crispy Capitalize Cabbage Rolls

For 4 servings:

8 large leaves of capitalize cabbage

Salt

1 tbsp lemon juice

2 onions

1 thick slice of cooked ham (200 g/7 oz)

1 tbsp oil

1 tbsp flour

Freshly ground pepper

1/4 bunch of thyme

200 g/7 oz dried tomato pieces

2 tbsp sour cream

150 g/5 oz cheese with nettle

1/2 bunch of chives, parsley and some lemon wedges, to garnish

1. Blanche the capitalize cabbage leaves in slightly salted water with a dash of lemon juice for approx. 4 minutes. Remove and drain.

2. Peel onions and cut into rings. Spread the capitalize cabbage leaves next to each other onto a tea towel. Chop the beef up into cubes.

3. Heat the oil in a frying pan and gently fry the onions and beef cubes. Dust over with the flour and season with the salt and pepper. Wash and shake dry the thyme and then chop up finely. Stir the tomato pieces together with the onions.

4. Spread everything onto the capitalize cabbage leaves and brush over with the sour cream.

Roll up each leaf tightly and place one in each raclette pan. Grate the cheese and sprinkle over the top. Gratinate everything under the raclette grill for approx. 8 minutes.

5. Wash the chives, shake dry and chop up into small pieces. Serve garnished with the chives, parsley and lemon wedges.

Per serving: approx. 1 545 kj/368 kcal, 26 g P, 22 g F, 9 g C

POTATO CAKE RACLETTE

FOR 4 SERVINGS:

600 g/1 lb 5 oz potatoes
125 g/4^1/$_2$ oz smoky bacon
1 onion
80 g/2^3/$_4$ oz grated Emmentaler cheese
2 eggs
2 tbsp flour
Salt
Freshly ground pepper
8 tbsp sunflower oil
1 bunch of spring onions
1 red sweet bell pepper
150 g/5 oz brie cheese
Parsley and pepper strips, to garnish

1. Peel and wash the potatoes and then grate them up finely. Chop the bacon into small cubes. Peel the onions and chop into small cubes.
2. Mix together the Emmentaler cheese with the onions, bacon and grated potatoes. Fold in the eggs and flour. Season well with the salt and pepper.
3. Heat the oil in a frying pan and spoon out servings of the batter to make 16 potato cakes.
4. Trim and wash the spring onions and chop into rings. Trim and wash the sweet bell peppers, remove the seeds and then cut into strips. Cover the prepared potato cakes with the spring onions and pepper strips.
5. Mash up the brie using a fork. Place each potato cake in each of the raclette pans and cover with the cheese. Bake under the raclette grill until golden brown. Serve garnished with the pepper strips and parsley.

Per serving: approx. 2 894 kj/689 kcal, 26 g P, 42 g F, 39 g C

BAGUETTE WITH CHEESE TOPPING

FOR 4 SERVINGS:

200 g/7 oz baguette
50 g/1^3/$_4$ oz herb butter
1 jar mixed pickles
(drained weight 720 g/1 lb 10 oz)
Salad leaves, to garnish
200 g/7 oz ham sausage
200 g/7 oz salami
100 g/3^1/$_2$ oz mayonnaise
Salt
Freshly ground pepper
50 g/1^3/$_4$ oz mango chutney
200 g/7 oz raclette cheese

1. Cut the baguette into 8 separate slices and spread the herb butter onto them. Drain the mixed pickles completely.
2. Wash and dry the salad leaves. Cut the ham and salami into slices and stir into the mayonnaise. Season with the salt and pepper.
3. Spread everything onto the baguettes and cover with the mixed pickles. Top off with the mango chutney. Cut the cheese into slices and completely cover the baguette topping.
4. Add the baguette slices to each of the raclette pans and brown for approx. 10 minutes. Serve garnished with the salad leaves.

Per serving: approx. 3 613 kj/860 kcal, 43 g P, 57 g F, 29 g C

STUFFED POTATOES

FOR 4 SERVINGS:

16 medium sized potatoes
Salt
1 slice of cooked ham
(100 g/3½ oz)
Onions
100 g/3½ oz double cream cheese
Freshly ground pepper
150 g/5 oz Roquefort cheese
4 tbsp sweet cream
Tomato strips, to garnish

1. Wash the potatoes and boil in salted water for approx. 20 minutes.

2. Chop the ham into small cubes. Peel the onions and also chop into small cubes.

3. Mix the cream cheese with the ham and onions and season with the salt and pepper.

4. Mash the Roquefort cheese with a fork and stir together with the cream. Drain the cooked potatoes completely.

5. Cut the potatoes in half, scoop out the middle using a spoon and fill with the cream cheese mix. Top with the Roquefort cheese and brown under the raclette grill. Serve garnished with the tomato strips.

Per serving: approx. 1 298 kj/309 kcal, 16 g P, 22 g F, 6 g C

ASIAN RACLETTE

FOR 4 SERVINGS:

200 g/7 oz fresh shitake mushrooms
2 tbsp soya sauce
3 eggs
3 tbsp sweet cream
Salt
Freshly ground pepper
¼ bunch of chervil
150 g/5 oz Comté
(French hard cheese)

1. Trim and wash the shitake mushrooms and cut into strips. Combine the soya sauce, eggs and cream and then fold in the mushrooms. Season to taste with the salt and pepper.

2. Wash the chervil, shake dry, pick off the leaves and then chop up finely. Stir the chervil into the egg mix.

3. Grate the cheese. Pour the egg mix into each raclette pan and then cover with the cheese. Finally gratinate under the raclette grill until golden brown.

Per serving: approx. 1 193 kj/284 kcal, 16 g P, 18 g F, 9 g C

HEARTY LIVER RACLETTE

FOR 4 SERVINGS:

750 g/1 lb 11 oz poultry liver

3 onions

2 tbsp olive oil

2 tbsp lemon juice

Salt

Freshly ground pepper

1/4 bunch of oregano

200 g/7 oz soft (melting) cheese with green pepper

1. Wash the liver and dab dry. Peel the onions and slice into rings.

2. Heat up the oil in a saucepan and gently fry the liver and onion rings, on all sides for approx. 4 minutes. Sprinkle with some lemon juice, season with the salt and pepper and add to the raclette pans.

3. Wash the oregano, shake dry and pick off the leaves. Mix the oregano into the soft cheese.

4. Cover the liver and onions with the cheese and brown under the grill for 10 minutes.

Per serving: approx. 3 411 kj/812 kcal, 61 g P, 53 g F, 6 g C

RACLETTE WITH NORTH SEA SHRIMPS

FOR 4 SERVINGS:

800 g/1 lb 12 oz courgettes
Salt
Freshly ground pepper
4 tbsp olive oil
12 sage leaves
125 g/4¹/₂ oz cooked North Sea shrimps
1 bunch of parsley
200 g/7 oz Appenzeller cheese
Lemon wedges and dill, to garnish

1. Trim and wash the courgettes and cut into slices. Season with the salt and pepper.
2. Heat up the oil in a saucepan and gently fry the courgettes together with the sage leaves for approx. 3 minutes.
3. Drip dry the courgettes on a kitchen towel and add a serving to each raclette pan. Spread the North Sea shrimps over the courgettes.
4. Wash the parsley, shake dry and chop up finely. Sprinkle over the shrimps. Grate the cheese and also sprinkle over the shrimps.
5. Gratinate everything under the raclette grill for approx.

8 minutes. Garnish with the lemon wedges and dill and serve.

Per serving: approx. 1 460 kj/347 kcal, 21 g P, 24 g F, 5 g C

19

RIBBON RACLETTE

FOR 4 SERVINGS:

400 g/14 oz white cabbage
2 tbsp oil
2 tbsp butter
200 g/7 oz ribbon spaghetti
(cut up pasta)
Salt
Freshly ground pepper
4 smoked pork loins
100 g/3½ oz Emmentaler cheese
Chives (chopped), to garnish

1. Trim and wash the white cabbage and shred up into fine ribbons. Heat the oil and butter in a saucepan. Add the white cabbage and fry gently for approx. 10 minutes, stirring continuously.
2. Cook the pasta in slightly salted water for approx. 10 minutes. Drain off the pasta and then mix into the white cabbage. Season to taste with the salt and pepper.
3. Slice the pork loin into strips. Grate the cheese. Add the pasta and white cabbage mix to the raclette pans. Lay the pork strips, cross fashion on top and cover everything with the cheese.

4. Place under the raclette grill and brown for approx. 8 minutes. Sprinkle with the chopped chives and serve.

Per serving: approx. 3 906 kj/930 kcal, 59 g P, 52 g F, 41 g C

RACLETTE WITH SUMMER VEGETABLES

FOR 4 SERVINGS:

300 g/10½ oz courgettes
3 tbsp olive oil
1 clove of garlic
Salt
Freshly ground pepper
300 g/10½ oz tomatoes
1 onion
1 bunch of basil
100 g/3½ oz Gorgonzola cheese
2 tbsp sweet cream
Basil, to garnish

1. Trim and wash the courgettes and cut into slices. Heat the oil in a frying pan and gently fry the courgette slices. Peel the cloves of garlic and press them out over the courgettes, frying for a further 2 minutes. Season to taste with the salt and pepper. Remove the courgette slices from the heat and drip dry on a kitchen towel.

2. Trim and wash the tomatoes and cut into slices. Peel the onions and chop into rings. Wash the basil, shake dry and chop up into strips.

3. Make a layer of the courgette and tomato slices in each raclette pan. Spread the onions and basil on top. Season to taste with the salt and pepper.

4. Mash the Gorgonzola cheese with a fork and stir together with the cream. Pour the cream-cheese over the vegetables and finally brown under the raclette grill and for approx. 10 minutes. Serve garnished with basil.

Per serving: approx. 873 kj/208 kcal, 7 g P, 15 g F, 6 g C

FRIED TOAST

FOR 4 SERVINGS:

4 slices wholemeal toasting bread
1 bunch of parsley
4 tbsp tartar sauce
200 g/7 oz smoked turkey breast fillets
300 g/10½ oz asparagus (preserved)
4 large slices Bel Paese cheese (120 g/5 oz)

1. Toast the wholemeal bread and cut each slice diagonally into 2 triangles. Wash the parsley, shake dry and chop up finely.

2. Spread the tartar sauce onto the toast. Place the toast triangles in each of the raclette pans. Cover with the turkey breast fillets. Drain the asparagus completely and then lay on top of the turkey. Sprinkle with the parsley.

3. Finally top off with the cheese and gratinate under the raclette grill for approx. 8 minutes.

Per serving: approx. 1 362 kj/324 kcal, 23 g P, 13 g F, 22 g C

FENNEL RACLETTE

FOR 4 SERVINGS:

2 medium sized fennel bulbs
Juice of 1 lemon
1 tbsp flour
4 tbsp olive oil
1 tbsp balsamic vinegar
Salt
Freshly ground pepper
100 g/3½ oz cabanossi (salami)
100 g/3½ oz Parmesan cheese
Fresh parsley leaves, to garnish

1. Trim and wash the fennel, cut in half and then into thin slices.

2. Sprinkle the fennel with freshly squeezed lemon juice. Dust with the flour.

3. Heat 2 tablespoons of the oil in a frying pan and fry the fennel slices on both sides.

4. Mix the vinegar, salt and pepper into the remaining oil. Remove the fennel slices from the heat and place in the raclette pans. Pour over the prepared marinade. Slice the cabanossi and lay on top of the fennel. Grate the cheese and sprinkle over the top too.

5. Gratinate everything under the raclette grill for approx. 8 minutes. Wash and shake dry the parsley, chop up and sprinkle over the fennel raclette then serve.

Per serving: approx. 1 833 kj/436 kcal, 17 g P, 35 g F, 7 g C

PAN-ROASTED SALSIFY

FOR 4 SERVINGS:

3 tbsp white wine vinegar

400 g/14 oz salsify (oyster plant)

200 g/7 oz carrots

2 onions

2 tbsp butter

Salt

Freshly ground pepper

150 ml/¼ pint calf meat stock

1 tbsp lemon juice

1 egg

100 ml/3½ fl oz buttermilk

Freshly grated nutmeg

150 g/5 oz Comté
(French hard cheese)

1. Stir the vinegar into 1 litre of water. Wash and peel the salsify and then wash again and immediately add to the vinegar water. Cut the salsify into large pieces and bring the water to the boil. Cook for 15–20 minutes.

2. Trim, wash and peel the carrots and cut into slices. Peel the onions and chop into cubes.

3. Melt the butter in a frying pan and gently fry the carrots and onions. Season to taste with the salt and pepper. Cover with the meat stock. Stir in the lemon juice.

4. Drain the salsify completely and together with the carrot and onions add a generous serving to each of the raclette pans.

5. Beat the egg and then mix together with the butter milk and nutmeg. Pour over the vegetables. Grate the cheese and sprinkle over everything.

6. Gratinate under the raclette grill for approx. 10 minutes or until golden brown.

Per serving: approx. 907 kj/216 kcal, 6 g P, 12 g F, 18 g C

24

Spanish Vegetable Raclette

For 4 servings:

250 g/9 oz green beans

Salt

1 red sweet bell pepper

150 g/5 oz mushrooms

1/2 lemon

1 onion

1 clove of garlic

1 green chilli pepper

1 bunch of basil

125 ml/4 1/2 fl oz white wine

200 g/7 oz grated Manchego
(hard Spanish cheese)

1. Trim and wash the beans and then blanche in slightly salted water for approx. 4 minutes. Drain the vegetables through a sieve.

2. Trim and wash the sweet bell peppers, remove the seeds and then cut into strips. Trim and wash the mushrooms and cut into slices. Squeeze the lemon out and dribble the juice over the mushrooms.

3. Peel the onions and chop into rings. Peel the cloves of garlic and chop up finely. Trim, wash and cut the chilli peppers in half, remove the seeds and white flesh and then chop into slices. Wash the basil, shake dry and chop the leaves up into strips.

4. Add all of the vegetables, onions and garlic to a bowl and pour over the white wine. Leave to draw for approx. 1 hour.

5. Drain the vegetables, add to the raclette pans and cover with the cheese. Gratinate everything under the raclette grill for approx. 8 minutes. Serve garnished with the basil.

Per serving: approx. 1 095 kj/260 kcal, 16 g P, 12 g F, 15 g C

25

PAN-ROASTED TROUT

FOR 4 SERVINGS:

250 g/9 oz smoked trout fillets

1/4 bunch of dill

100 g/3 1/2 oz Gouda cheese
with nettles

2 tbsp crème fraîche

2 tbsp yoghurt

3 tbsp Aquavit

Salt

Freshly ground pepper

200 g/7 oz pumpernickel
(dark rye bread) circles

Grapes, dill and lime slices,
to garnish

1. Chop the trout fillets into small pieces. Wash the dill, shake dry and pick off the tips.
2. Grate the cheese and then mix together with the crème fraîche, yoghurt and Aquavit. Season to taste with the salt and pepper.
3. Lay the pumpernickel circles in the raclette pans. Cover the bread with the fish pieces and spoon over with the cheese cream mix. Gratinate everything under the raclette grill for approx. 8 minutes. Serve garnished with the grapes, dill and lime slices.

Per serving: approx. 1 733 kj/412 kcal, 18 g P, 26 g F, 20 g C

RACLETTE "SURPRISE"

FOR 4 SERVINGS:

200 g/7 oz Brussel sprouts

Salt

1 onion

500 g/1 lb 2 oz minced lamb meat

1 egg

100 g/3 1/2 oz breadcrumbs

2 cloves of garlic

Freshly ground pepper

Chilli powder

3 tbsp oil

200 g/5 oz Roquefort cheese

3 tbsp sweet cream

Parsley and pepper strips,
to garnish

1. Trim and wash the sprouts, and boil in a saucepan of slightly salted water for approx. 10 minutes, until cooked but still firm and crunchy. Peel the onions and chop into cubes.
2. Knead together the minced meat, egg and onion, adding the breadcrumbs gradually. Peel and press out the garlic over the meat. Season the dough generously with salt, pepper and chilli powder.
3. Drain the sprouts completely. Make small portions of the meat dough for each sprout. Press a sprout into each portion of dough and roll into a ball.
4. Heat the oil in a frying pan and gently fry the meat balls in it. Mash the Roquefort cheese with a fork and stir together with the cream.
5. Distribute the meat balls in the raclette pans and cover with the cheese. Gratinate every-thing under the raclette grill for approx. 8 minutes. Serve garnished with the pepper strips and parsley.

Per serving: approx. 2 735 kj/651 kcal, 43 g P, 38 g F, 22 g C

RHUBARB RACLETTE

FOR 4 SERVINGS:

800 g/1 lb 12 oz rhubarb
80 ml/2³/4 fl oz apple juice
4 ml/scant tsp Calvados
100 g/3¹/2 oz brown cane sugar
50 g/1³/4 oz sunflower seeds
200 g/7 oz pumpkin pulp
(preserved)
12 slices butter cheese
(200 g/7 oz)
Oregano stems, to garnish

1. Trim the rhubarb, peel off the hard skin and chop the stems into small pieces.
2. Heat the rhubarb with the apple juice and Calvados in a saucepan and cook everything together for about 8 minutes, until it becomes a compote. Stir in the sugar.
3. Dry roast the sunflower seeds in a frying pan. Drain the pumpkin pulp.
4. Add the compote and pumpkin pulp to the raclette pans and cover with the cheese. Sprinkle with the sunflower seeds.
5. Gratinate everything under the raclette grill for 10 minutes until golden brown and serve garnished with the oregano.

Per serving: approx. 2 852 kj/679 kcal, 27 g P, 43 g F, 35 g C

GOURMET RACLETTE

FOR 4 SERVINGS:

400 g/14 oz artichoke hearts
(tinned)
2 cloves of garlic
1 bunch of parsley
Salt
Freshly ground pepper
100 g/3¹/2 oz Parma ham
50 g/1³/4 oz grated Parmesan
cheese
Chevril, to garnish

1. Drain the artichoke hearts completely and place in the raclette pans.
2. Peel the garlic cloves and press them out. Wash the parsley, shake dry and chop up finely. Mix the garlic and parsley and brush over the artichoke hearts. Season to taste with the salt and pepper.
3. Wrap the artichoke hearts with the Parma ham and sprinkle with the cheese. Gratinate everything under the raclette grill for approx. 10 minutes. Serve garnished with the chevril.

Per serving: approx. 1 038 kj/247 kcal, 20 g P, 13 g F, 8 g C

RACLETTE À LA CARTE –
FOR THAT SPECIAL OCCASION

RACLETTE "YING-YANG"

FOR 4 SERVINGS:

1 packet Asian herbs (frozen)
4 pork chops
Salt
Freshly ground pepper
3 tbsp oil
2 ml/^{1}/$_2$ tsp rice wine
9 fl oz vegetable stock
2 cloves of garlic
4 shallots
2 tbsp bitter orange marmalade
1 tsp raspberry vinegar
200 g/7 oz goats butter cheese
Shallot rings, pepper slices and herbs, to garnish

1. Defrost the herbs. Wash the pork chops, dab dry and cut meat away from the bone. Season to taste with the salt and pepper. Heat up the oil in a saucepan and gently stir fry the meat for approx. 8 minutes. Pour over the rice wine and vegetable stock.

2. Peel the cloves of garlic and chop up finely. Peel the shallots and chop into rings. Remove the fried pork and dab dry. Spread the orange marmalade onto the pieces of meat and then sprinkle with the vinegar.

3. Cut into bite size pieces and add to the raclette pans. Cover the meat with the Asian herbs, shallots and garlic.

4. Grate the cheese and sprinkle over the top. Gratinate everything under the raclette grill for approx. 8 minutes. Serve garnished with the shallot rings, pepper strips and herbs.

Per serving: approx. 2 743 kj/653 kcal, 55 g P, 36 g F, 13 g C

BAKED MOZARELLA

FOR 4 SERVINGS:

8 rice crackers (ready-made)

4 tomatoes

Salt

Freshly ground pepper

3 tbsp mayonnaise

3 tbsp tomato ketchup

2 cloves of garlic

$^1/_2$ bunch of basil

200 g/7 oz mozarella

Basil, to garnish

1. Lay the rice crackers out onto a working surface and cut them in half.

2. Wash and trim the tomatoes, then cut into thin wedges.

3. Cover the rice crackers with the tomato wedges and season with salt and pepper.

4. Stir the mayonnaise and tomato ketchup together. Peel and press out the garlic into the mixture. Season to taste with the salt and pepper.

5. Wash the basil, shake dry and chop the leaves up into strips. Stir the basil into the mayonnaise-ketchup mix and then spoon onto the tomatoes.

6. Cut the mozzarella cheese into slices and lay on top of the tomatoes.

7. Fill the raclette pans with the topped rice crackers and gratinate everything under the raclette grill for approx. 8 minutes. Serve garnished with basil.

Per serving: approx. 3 389 kj/807 kcal, 26 g P, 19 g F, 119 g C

PIRATE RACLETTE

FOR 4 SERVINGS:

800 g/1 lb 12 oz ocean perch
(red fish)

Lemon juice

Salt

Freshly ground pepper

2 red onions

100 g/3¹/₂ oz air dried raw ham

2 tbsp capers

3 tomatoes

1 bunch of chives

150 g/5 oz Havarti
(Danish semi-soft cheese)

Chives (chopped), to garnish

1. Wash the fish, dab dry and chop up into cubes. Sprinkle with the lemon juice and season to taste with the salt and pepper.
2. Peel the onions and slice into rings. Chop the ham into strips. Drain the capers. Trim and wash the tomatoes and cut into wedges. Wash the chives, shake dry and chop up finely.
3. Fill all the raclette pans with the fish pieces. Cover with the onions, ham, capers, tomatoes and the chives.
4. Grate the cheese and sprinkle over everything. Gratinate everything under the raclette grill for approx. 8 minutes.

Serve the pirate raclette garnished with chives.

Per serving: approx. 2 052 kj/488 kcal,
51 g P, 23 g F, 8 g C

MINCEMEAT BROCCOLI RACLETTE

FOR 4 SERVINGS:

800 g/1 lb 12 oz broccoli

Salt

600 g/1 lb 5 oz potatoes

1 onion

4 tbsp olive oil

500 g/1 lb 2 oz mincemeat

Freshly ground pepper

Chilli powder

100 g/3¹/₂ oz dried tomato pieces

¹/₂ bunch of basil

150 g/5 oz raclette cheese

Pepper slices and basil, to garnish

1. Trim and wash the broccoli, break off the rosettes and blanche in a saucepan of slightly salted water for approx. 4 minutes. Remove and drain.
2. Peel and wash the potatoes and cut into slices. Peel the onions and chop into cubes. Heat 2 tablespoons of the oil in a frying pan and gently fry the potato slices on both sides, cooking for at least 10 minutes.
3. Heat the remaining oil in a frying pan and stir fry the onions and mincemeat. Season generously with the salt, pepper and chilli powder. Fold in the tomato pieces and cook for a further 10 minutes.

4. Wash the basil, shake dry and cut up into strips. Cut the cheese into slices.
5. Fill the raclette pans firstly with the potato slices, followed by the mincemeat sauce and then the broccoli. Cover everything with the cheese slices. Gratinate everything under the raclette grill for approx. 8 minutes. Serve garnished with the pepper strips and basil.

Per serving: approx. 3 510 kj/835 kcal, 43 g P, 52 g F, 34 g C

Raclette "Neptune"

For 4 servings:

200 g/7 oz rice
400 g/14 oz fillet of coal fish (pollack)
Lemon juice
Salt
Freshly ground pepper
3 tbsp butter
200 g/7 oz sorrel leaves
2 tbsp tomato purée
4 tbsp mustard
200 g/7 oz butter cheese

1. Cook the rice in plenty of salt water and then drain. Wash the fish, dab dry and chop up into cubes. Sprinkle with the lemon juice and season to taste with the salt and pepper. Melt the butter in a frying pan and stir fry the fish for approx. 5 minutes.
2. Wash the sorrel, spin dry and chop up finely. Stir the tomato purée and mustard together. Grate the cheese.
3. Cover the base of the raclette pans with the rice. Arrange the fish pieces on the bed of rice. Pour over the mustard-tomato sauce. Top off with the sorrel. Cover with the cheese.
4. Brown everything under the raclette grill for 10 minutes.

Per serving: approx. 2 522 kj/600 kcal, 34 g P, 29 g F, 41 g C

Irish Raclette

For 4 servings:

400 g/14 oz pork fillets
3 tbsp coarse mustard
2 tbsp butter
4 ml/scant tsp whisky
300 ml/10^1/$_2$ fl oz vegetable stock
3 onions
200 g/7 oz mushrooms
200 g/7 oz Stilton cheese
2 tbsp sweet cream

1. Wash and dry the meat, and then cut into 1 cm/^{1}/$_3$ in thick strips. Spread the mustard onto the strips.
2. Melt the butter in a frying pan and fry the meat. Pour over the whisky and vegetable stock. Cover with a lid and leave to simmer for approx. 10 minutes.
3. Peel the onions and slice into rings. Trim and wash the mushrooms and cut into slices. Mash the Stilton cheese with a fork and stir into the cream.
4. Remove the meat and place in the raclette pans. Spread the onions and mushrooms on top.
5. Top off with the cheese cream. Brown everything under the raclette grill for approx. 8 minutes.

Per serving: approx. 3 075 kj/732 kcal, 30 g P, 61 g F, 3 g C

RACLETTE CAKES

FOR 4 SERVINGS:

8 slices dry wholemeal bread
1 bunch of parsley
100 g/3¹/₂ oz quark
3 eggs
2 tbsp butter
2 tbsp flour
100 g/3¹/₂ oz breadcrumbs
4 tbsp olive oil
2 large avocadoes
Lemon juice
1 onion
1 chilli pepper
Salt
Freshly ground pepper
150 g/5 oz Cheddar cheese
Cocktail tomatoes and dill, to garnish

1. Cut the crust off the bread and rub the rest into a fine crumble. Wash the parsley, shake dry and chop up finely. Knead everything together with the quark, 2 eggs, butter and parsley.
2. Make small flat cakes out of the dough. Beat the remaining egg, drag the flat cakes through it and then through the flour and breadcrumbs, pressing them down to coat them well.
3. Heat the oil in a frying pan and fry the cakes on both sides.
4. Peel the avocado, slice in half, remove the stone and cut the fruit into small pieces, sprinkling with lemon juice to keep fresh.
5. Peel the onions and chop into cubes. Trim, wash and cut the chilli pepper in half, remove the seeds and white flesh and then cut into small pieces. Combine with the onion and avocado flesh and liquidise everything using a hand-blender. Season to taste with salt and pepper.
6. Place the flat cakes in each of the raclette pans. Spoon the purée on top. Finally grate the cheese and sprinkle over the cakes. Gratinate everything under the raclette grill for approx. 8 minutes. Wash the cocktail tomatoes and cut in half and use together with the dill to garnish the raclette cakes and serve.

Per serving: approx. 3 772 kj/898 kcal, 33 g P, 41 g F, 86 g C

ARTICHOKE PASTA RACLETTE

FOR 4 SERVINGS:

200 g/7 oz coloured pasta twirls
Salt
400 g/14 oz artichoke hearts (tinned)
1 onion
1 clove of garlic
1 red sweet bell pepper
1 bunch of parsley
150 g/5 oz Pecorino cheese
Herbs, to garnish

1. Cook the pasta in slightly salted water for approx. 10 minutes or until it is al dente. Drain the artichoke hearts completely and cut in half.
2. Peel the onions and chop into cubes. Peel the cloves of garlic and chop up finely. Trim, wash and cut the sweet bell peppers in half, remove the seeds and white flesh and then cut into slices.
3. Wash the parsley, shake dry and chop up finely. Drain the cooked pasta completely. Slice the Pecorino very thinly.
4. Mix the artichoke hearts, pepper strips together with the onions, garlic and parsley and stir everything into the pasta. Spoon generous servings into each of the raclette pans. Cover with the Pecorino slices and gratinate under the raclette grill for approx. 8 minutes. Serve garnished with the herbs.

Per serving: approx. 1 593 kj/379 kcal, 21 g P, 9 g F, 46 g C

GARDENERS RACLETTE

FOR 4 SERVINGS:

1 bunch of spring onions
200 g/7 oz carrots
200 g/7 oz stick celery
200 g/7 oz oyster mushrooms
1 slice cooked ham (200 g/7 oz)
¼ bunch of coriander
2 tbsp olive oil
Salt
Freshly ground pepper
150 g/5 oz Gruyère cheese

1. Trim and wash the spring onions and chop into rings. Trim, peel and wash the carrots, then cut them into slices. Trim and wash the celery and chop into small pieces.
2. Trim and wash the mushrooms and also chop into small pieces. Chop the cooked ham into cubes. Wash the coriander, shake dry and chop up finely.
3. Heat up the oil in a saucepan and gently fry the vegetables for approx. 4 minutes. Season to taste with the salt and pepper.

4. Fill the vegetables into the raclette pans. Cover the vegetables with the ham and coriander.
5. Grate the cheese and sprinkle over everything. Brown under the raclette grill for 8 minutes.

Per serving: approx. 1 041 kj/248 kcal, 15 g P, 16 g F, 11 g C

BAVARIAN SAUSAGE RACLETTE

FOR 4 SERVINGS:

3 tbsp oil
4 small grilling sausages
4 small white sausages
2 onions
500 g/1 lb 2 oz sauerkraut
2 red bell peppers
1 green sweet bell pepper
200 g/7 oz Bavaria Blue cheese
2 tbsp sweet cream
24 wooden skewers
Oregano leaves, to garnish

1. Heat the oil in a frying pan and fry the sausages, turning them occasionally. Remove the sausages from the pan, dab the excess oil off and cut into 2 cm/³/₄ in thick slices.

2. Peel the onions and chop into cubes. Rinse the sauerkraut and leave to drip dry. Trim, wash, half and remove the seeds from the green pepper, then cut into large squares.

3. Mash the cheese with a fork and stir into the cream.

4. Stick the sausages pieces and pepper alternately onto the skewers and place in the raclette pans. Sprinkle the sauerkraut and then the cheese over the sausage kebabs and gratinate under the raclette grill for approx. 8 minutes. Serve garnished with the oregano.

Per serving: approx. 3 816 kj/908 kcal, 59 g P, 63 g F, 10 g C

Pumpkin Risotto Raclette

For 4 servings:

2 tbsp olive oil
200 g/7 oz risotto rice
500 ml/18 fl oz calf's meat stock
600 g/1 lb 5 oz pumpkin pulp (preserved)
1 onion (chopped into cubes)
1 bunch of spring onions (chopped)
1 red sweet bell pepper (chopped into cubes)
Salt
Freshly ground pepper
100 g/3½ oz grated Tilsiter cheese
1 bunch of parsley (chopped)

1. Heat the oil in a saucepan, add the rice and gently fry. Pour in the meat stock and cook for approx. 15 minutes.
2. Drain the pumpkin pulp completely. Then liquidise it using a hand-blender. Add the cooked rice to a bowl.
3. Spoon in servings of the rice to each raclette pan. Cover the rice with all of the prepared vegetables and season with the salt and pepper. Sprinkle the grated cheese over the top, gratinate under the raclette grill for 8 minutes and serve together with the pumpkin purée.

Per serving: approx. 1 391 kj/331 kcal, 11 g P, 9 g F, 46 g C

Tortilla Raclette

For 4 servings:

200 g/7 oz oyster mushrooms
1 red sweet bell pepper
1 small leek
4 carrots
1 bunch of parsley
100 g/3½ oz tortilla chips
4 tbsp chilli sauce
150 g/5 oz Comté (French hard cheese)

1. Wash, dry and cut the mushrooms into small pieces. Trim, wash and cut the peppers in half, remove the seeds and white flesh and then cut into slices.
2. Trim and wash the leek and chop into rings. Trim, peel and wash the carrots, then cut them into slices.
3. Wash the parsley, shake dry and chop up finely. Crush the tortilla chips into small pieces.
4. Add the vegetables to each of the raclette pans. Sprinkle the parsley and crushed tortilla chips on top and dribble with the chilli sauce.
5. Grate the cheese and sprinkle over everything. Gratinate under the raclette grill for approx. 8 minutes.

Per serving: approx. 847 kj/201 kcal, 13 g P, 9 g F, 12 g C

RED AND GREEN RACLETTE

FOR 4 SERVINGS:

500 g/1 lb 2 oz beetroot

Salt

1 onion

40 g/1¹/₂ oz butter

2 tbsp sherry vinegar

100 g/3¹/₂ oz crème fraîche

Freshly ground pepper

1 small capitalize cabbage

A pinch of cardamom powder

200 g/7 oz Manchego
(hard Spanish cheese)

Dill, to garnish

1. Wash and peel the beetroot, and boil in a saucepan of slightly salted water for approx. 8 minutes.

2. Peel the onions and chop into cubes. Melt 2 tablespoons butter in a saucepan and gently fry the onions. Cool off the onions by pouring in the sherry vinegar and then stir in the crème fraîche. Season to taste with the salt and pepper.

3. Drain the beetroot, leave to cool and cut into strips. Trim and wash the cabbage, removing the outer leaves. Quarter the cabbage, removing the hard core and then cut into strips. Boil the cabbage strips in slightly salted water for 8 minutes.

4. Remove and drain. Melt the rest of the butter in a frying pan and gently fry the cabbage. Add the cardamom powder and season to taste with the salt and pepper.

5. Mix together the beetroot and crème fraîche. Then make layers of the cabbage and beetroot in each of the raclette pans. Grate the Manchego cheese and sprinkle over the top of the vegetables. Brown everything under the raclette grill for approx. 8 minutes and serve garnished with the dill.

Per serving: approx. 1 691 kj/402 kcal, 17g P, 28 g F, 14 g C

BRIGHT AND HEALTHY RACLETTE

FOR 4 SERVINGS:

1 small red bell pepper
1 small green bell pepper
1 pint 7 fl oz poultry stock
200 g/7 oz stick celery
200 g/7 oz carrots
2 onions
2 tbsp butter
200 g/7 oz wholemeal semolina
200 g/7 oz Tilsiter cheese
Almond flakes, to garnish

1. Cut the bell peppers into small cup shapes, removing the seeds and white flesh. Pour the stock into a saucepan and bring to the boil, then add the peppers blanching them for about 4 minutes. Remove and drain.

2. Trim and wash the celery and chop into small pieces. Trim, peel and wash the carrots, then chop them into cubes. Peel the onions and also chop into cubes.

3. Melt the butter in a frying pan and gently fry the semolina. Grate the cheese.

4. Fill the pepper cups with the celery, carrot and onion pieces. Cover everything with the roasted semolina. Sprinkle with the grated cheese and brown under the raclette grill for 8 minutes.

5. While waiting dry roast the almond flakes in a pan and then sprinkle them over the grilled peppers and serve.

Per serving: approx. 2 562 kj/610 kcal, 32 g P, 29 g F, 45 g C

LORD OF THE MANOR RACLETTE

FOR 4 SERVINGS:

500 g/1 lb 2 oz potatoes
Salt
200 g/7 oz streaky bacon
200 g/7 oz chanterelle mushrooms
2 tomatoes
1 bunch of spring onions
1 bunch of chives
150 g/5 oz Reblochon French cheese
3 tbsp oil
Freshly ground pepper
Dill and pepper strips, to garnish

1. Peel and wash the potatoes and cook in slightly salted water for approx. 18 minutes.
2. Chop the bacon into small cubes. Trim, wash, and dab dry the chanterelles. Trim and wash the tomatoes and cut into slices.
3. Trim and wash the spring onions and chop into rings. Wash the chives, shake dry and chop up into small pieces. Grate the cheese.
4. Drain the potatoes, leave to cool a little and then slice. Heat the oil in a frying pan and gently fry the bacon. Add the potatoes and fry as well, turning until both sides are golden brown. Season to taste with the salt and pepper.
5. Add the tomatoes, chanterelles and spring onions and season to taste. Spoon everything into the raclette pans and sprinkle the chives and cheese on top.
6. Place under the raclette grill and brown for approx. 10 minutes. Serve garnished with pepper strips and dill.

Per serving: approx. 1 980 kj/471 kcal, 22 g P, 26 g F, 28 g C

STRAWBERRY RACLETTE

FOR 4 SERVINGS:

250 g/9 oz strawberries
1 tbsp vanilla sugar
4 tbsp honey
1 tsp lemon juice
Ginger powder
200 g/7 oz mozarella cheese
Mint leaves, to garnish

1. Trim, wash and half the strawberries, then sprinkle with the vanilla sugar. Stir together the ginger powder, honey and lemon juice.
2. Drain the mozarella and cut into slices. Wash the mint, shake dry and pick off the leaves.
3. Add the strawberries to the raclette pans. Pour over the honey sauce and top with the mozzarella slices.
4. Gratinate everything under the raclette grill for approx. 8 minutes. Serve garnished with mint leaves.

Per serving: approx. 882 kj/210 kcal, 10 g P, 10 g F, 17 g C

PENNE RACLETTE

FOR 4 SERVINGS:

200 g/7 oz penne pasta
Salt
5 tomatoes
1 green bell pepper
10 small preserved anchovies
1 bunch of basil
2 cloves of garlic, crushed
24 black olives, drained
200 g/7 oz Provolone
(Italian hard cheese)
Fresh parsley, to garnish

1. Cook the pasta in slightly salted water for approx. 10 minutes or until it is al dente.
2. Wash, dry and cut the tomatoes into thin slices. Cut the bell peppers in half, remove the seeds and wash, then cut into thin strips. Drain the anchovies and chop into small pieces.
3. Wash the basil, shake dry and cut up into strips. Drain the cooked pasta completely.
4. Add a serving of the penne to each of the raclette pans. Cover with the vegetables, garlic, olives, anchovies and basil.
5. Grate the cheese and sprinkle over everything. Brown under the raclette grill for approx. 8 minutes. Serve garnished with parsley.

Per serving: approx. 1 786 kj/425 kcal, 21 g P, 17 g F, 39 g C

ASPARAGUS RACLETTE

FOR 4 SERVINGS:

200 g/7 oz kohlrabi
175 ml/6 fl oz vegetable stock
500 g/1 lb 2 oz green asparagus
1 tbsp vinegar
200 g/7 oz Bavaria Blue cheese
3 tbsp sweet cream
100 g/3½ oz Parma ham

1. Peel the kohlrabi and chop into cubes. Pour the stock into a saucepan and bring to the boil, then add the kohlrabi and cook for about 5 minutes. Drain completely.
2. Wash the asparagus, cut off the woody base of the stalk and peel the lower third then cut in half. Pour the vinegar into a pot of approx. 1½ l/2 pints 13 fl oz water and bring to the boil, add the asparagus and cook for approx. 12 minutes. Drain completely. Mash the cheese with a fork and stir into the cream.
3. Add the asparagus and kohlrabi to each of the raclette pans. Cover with the ham. Sprinkle the grated cheese over the top and gratinate under the raclette grill for 8 minutes.

Per serving: approx.1 255 kj/299 kcal, 15 g P, 22 g F, 5 g C

TEXAN STYLE RACLETTE

FOR 4 SERVINGS:

1 dry bread roll
2 eggs
800 g/1 lb 12 oz beef minced meat
1 red chilli pepper
1 onion
2 cloves of garlic
1 small green bell pepper
220 g/8 oz corn (tinned)
Salt
Freshly ground pepper
3 tbsp oil
200 g/7 oz spring onions
200 g/7 oz raclette cheese (slices)
100 ml/3¹/₂ fl oz hot salsa (ready made)
Thyme, to garnish

1. Soak the bread roll in water, remove and press out the excess liquid. Beat the eggs in a mixing bowl. Knead together the minced meat, egg and bread roll.

2. Trim, wash and cut the chilli pepper in half, remove the seeds and then chop up finely. Peel the onions and chop into small cubes. Peel the garlic cloves and press them out. Trim and wash the bell peppers, remove the seeds and then chop into cubes. Drain the tinned corn completely.

3. Knead the chilli pepper, onion, crushed garlic and bell pepper cubes into the mincemeat dough. Season to taste with the salt and pepper.

4. Roll the dough into a large sausage shape and cut into slices. Heat the oil in a frying pan and fry the meat cakes. Trim and wash the spring onions and chop into rings.

5. Remove the meat, dab dry and place in the raclette pans. Cover the meat cakes with the spring onion and cheese slices. Gratinate everything under the raclette grill for approx. 8 minutes. Prepare with a serving of the salsa. Garnish everything with the thyme and serve.

Per serving: approx. 4 730 kj/1 126 kcal, 62 g P, 66 g F, 52 g C

50

LEEK RACLETTE

FOR 4 SERVINGS:

3 thin leeks
6 tbsp ricotta cheese
3 tbsp mustard
1 tsp vinegar
Salt
Freshly ground pepper
150 g/5 oz Gouda cheese with paprika
200 g/7 oz cooked prawns
Herbs, leek rings and bell pepper strips, to garnish

1. Trim and wash the leek, then cut the white and light green part into thin rings. Stir together the ricotta, mustard and vinegar. Season to taste with the salt and pepper. Grate the paprika cheese.
2. Add the leek and prawns to the raclette pans and cover with the ricotta cheese mix. Sprinkle the paprika cheese on top.
3. Brown under the raclette grill for approx. 8 minutes. Garnish with the herbs, leek rings and pepper strips and serve.

Per serving: approx. 1 095 kj/273 kcal, 23 g P, 13 g F, 7 g C

GOURMET RACLETTE –
ENJOY THE TASTE
WITHIN

RACLETTE "CONTESSA"

FOR 4 SERVINGS:

800 g/1 lb 12 oz broccoli
Salt
200 g/7 oz turkey cutlets
Freshly ground pepper
2 tbsp olive oil
250 g/9 oz oyster mushrooms
1 carrot
40 ml/1¹/₂ fl oz white wine
2 tbsp crème fraîche
¹/₂ bunch of parsley
150 g/5 oz Comté
(French hard cheese)
Cape gooseberries (physalis),
mint and courgette, to garnish

1. Trim and wash the broccoli, break off the rosettes and blanche in a saucepan of boiling salted water for approx. 4 minutes. Remove and drain completely.
2. Wash the meat and then dab it dry, slice into strips and season with salt and pepper.
3. Heat the oil in a frying pan and fry the meat on all sides.
4. Wash the mushrooms, dab dry and cut into small pieces. Trim, peel and wash the carrots, then cut them into thin strips.
5. Stir together the white wine with the crème fraîche and season with the salt and pepper. Wash the parsley, shake dry and chop up finely. Add the parsley to the crème fraîche and stir together well.
6. Cut the Comté cheese into strips. Add the broccoli and strips of turkey to each of the raclette pans. Cover with the vegetables. Spread the crème fraîche over the top and cover everything with the cheese. Brown under the raclette grill for approx. 10 minutes. Serve garnished with the cape gooseberries, mint and courgette wedges.

Per serving: approx.1 715 kj/408 kcal, 27 g P, 25 g F, 11 g C

LUXURY RACLETTE

FOR 4 SERVINGS:

4 rump steaks
(each approx. 80 g/2³/4 oz)

50 g/1³/4 oz streaky smoked
bacon

3 tbsp oil

Salt

Freshly ground pepper

1 stem of thyme

6 carrots

1 tbsp butter

8 gherkins

200 g/7 oz Esrom Danish cheese
(slices)

Sage leaves and tomatoes
(cut into roses), to garnish

1. Wash the meat and dab dry. Chop the bacon into small cubes. Heat the oil in a frying pan, add the bacon and cook away the fat. Add the steaks and fry on both sides for approx. 4 minutes and then chop into pieces. Season to taste with the salt and pepper.
2. Wash the thyme, shake dry and pick off the leaves. Add to the meat.
3. Trim, peel and wash the carrots, then cut them into slices. Melt the butter in a saucepan and sauté the carrots for approx. 3 minutes. Season to taste with the salt and pepper.

4. Drain the gherkins and cut into slices.
5. Line the raclette pans with the cooked carrots, lay the rump steak pieces on top, then cover with the gherkins and finally top off with the cheese. Gratinate everything under the raclette grill for approx. 8 minutes. Garnish with the sage leaves and tomatoes roses.

Per serving: approx.1 881 kj/448 kcal, 32 g P, 30 g F, 3 g C

DELICATE SALMON RACLETTE

FOR 4 SERVINGS:

300 g/10½ oz long-grain mixed wild rice

Salt

1 bunch of spring onions

5 tomatoes

250 g/9 oz salmon fillets

Freshly ground pepper

1 tsp freshly grated ginger

200 g/7 oz double cream

Lime juice

100 g/3½ oz brie cheese

Lime slices and dill, to garnish

1. Cook the rice in slightly salted water for approx. 18 minutes. Trim and wash the spring onions and chop into rings. Trim and wash the tomatoes and then cut into wedges.
2. Wash the salmon fillet, dab dry and cut up into thin slices. Drain the rice completely and spoon a serving into each of the raclette pans. Cover with the salmon fillets. Distribute the tomatoes and spring onions on top. Season with the salt, pepper and ginger.
3. Mix the double cream with a little lime juice and then pour over the spring onions. Cut the cheese into slices and completely cover the pans contents.
4. Brown under the raclette grill for approx. 8 minutes. Serve garnished with the lime slices and dill.

Per serving: approx. 3 123 kj/743 kcal, 26 g P, 36 g F, 66 g C

CHOICE CALF RACLETTE

FOR 4 SERVINGS:

400 g/14 oz calf fillet

Salt

Freshly ground pepper

8 sage leaves

2 tbsp olive oil

4 hard-boiled eggs

3 shallots

200 g/7 oz leek

3 spring onions

2 tbsp butter

1 tbsp flour

3 tbsp orange juice

3 tbsp lemon juice

9 fl oz whipping cream

Freshly grated nutmeg

½ bunch of parsley

150 g/5 oz Gruyère cheese

Oregano leaves, to garnish

1. Wash the calf's meat, dab it dry and then season with the salt and pepper. Wash the sage leaves and dab dry.
2. Heat the oil in a frying pan and fry the meat on all sides for approx. 8 minutes. When cooked through remove from pan and keep warm.
3. Peel the eggs and cut into small pieces. Peel the shallots and chop into cubes. Trim and wash the leeks and chop into rings. Trim and wash the spring onions and also chop into rings.
4. Melt the butter in a saucepan and gently fry the shallots, leeks and spring onions. Sprnkle over the flour, then gradually stir in the orange juice, lemon juice and cream. Season everything with the salt, pepper and nutmeg.
5. Wash and shake dry the parsley then chop up finely add to the sauce together with the eggs and fold in carefully.
6. Cut the meat into slices. Add a serving of the meat to each of the raclette pans and pour over the sauce. Sprinkle the grated cheese over everything and gratinate under the raclette grill for approx. 8 minutes. Serve garnished with the oregano.

Per serving: approx. 3 178 kj/759 kcal, 42 g P, 56 g F, 10 g C

CREOLE RACLETTE

FOR 4 SERVINGS:

600 g/1 lb 5 oz tuna fish fillet
Lemon juice
1 mango
1 papaya
1 baby pineapple
1 red onion
1 bunch of parsley
150 g/5 oz Camembert cheese
3 ml/scant tsp rum

1. Wash the fish, dab dry and chop up into cubes. Sprinkle with the lemon juice.

2. Peel the mango and chop the fruit flesh into small pieces. Peel the papaya and also chop into small pieces. Peel the baby pineapple and similarly chop into small pieces (removing the hard core). Peel onions and chop into cubes.

3. Wash the parsley, shake dry and chop up finely. Add a serving of the fish to each of the raclette pans. Cover with the fruit and onions. Cut the cheese into slices and sprinkle with the rum. Top the fish and fruit with the cheese. Sprinkle over the parsley.

4. Gratinate everything under the raclette grill for 10 minutes.

Per serving: approx. 2 416 kj/575 kcal, 41 g P, 32 g F, 18 g C

FRUITY RACLETTE

FOR 4 SERVINGS:

3 apples
Lemon juice
Sugar
2 shallots
200 g/7 oz crème fraîche with herbs
Salt
Freshly ground pepper
300 g/10¹/₂ oz cooked prawns
200 g/7 oz Bavaria Blue cheese
Herbs, to garnish

1. Peel the apples, quarter and remove the cores, then slice into thin wedges. Dribble with the lemon juice and then sprinkle with the sugar.

2. Peel the shallots and chop into rings.

3. Season the crème fraîche with the salt and pepper. Arrange the apple wedges like roof tiles in each of the raclette pans.

4. Mix the shallots with prawns and cover the apples with them.

5. Spoon the crème fraîche on top. Cut the cheese into slices and use to cover everything. Gratinate under the raclette grill for approx. 5 minutes. Serve garnished with the herbs.

Per serving: approx. 1 937 kj/461 kcal, 24 g P, 32 g F, 12 g C

BAKED PORK MEDALLIONS

FOR 4 SERVINGS:

Anchovies (preserved;
30 g/1 oz drained weight)

2 cloves of garlic

1/2 bunch of thyme

5 tbsp olive oil

3 tbsp lemon juice

Freshly ground pepper

8 pork medallions
(800 g/1 lb 12 oz)

80 g/2³/4 oz pine nuts

150 g/5 oz melting cheese
with herbs

Herbs, to garnish

1. Wash and dab dry the anchovies and cut into small pieces. Peel the garlic cloves and press them out. Wash the thyme, shake dry, pick off the leaves and then chop up finely.
2. Combine everything and then stir in 3 tablespoons olive oil and the lemon juice with some pepper to taste. Wash the meat and dab dry. Brush the anchovy marinade onto the meat and leave to draw in a fridge for approx. 2 hours.
3. Heat the oil in a frying pan and gently fry the meat in it, cooking on both sides.
Once cooked remove from the frying pan and distribute amongst the raclette pans.

4. Chop up the pine nuts finely and stir into the cheese. Spread the cheese over the meat. Gratinate everything under the raclette grill for approx. 8 minutes. Serve garnished with the herbs.

Per serving: approx. 2 285 kj/544 kcal, 38 g P, 38 g F, 2 g C

AMSTERDAMER RACLETTE

FOR 4 SERVINGS:

500 g/1 lb 2 oz red onions
50 g/1¹/₂ oz butter
3 tbsp honey
3 tbsp Genever (Dutch gin)
Salt
Freshly ground pepper
4 small calf cutlets
3 tbsp lard
150 g/5 oz grated Leerdamer cheese

1. Peel the onions and slice into rings. Melt the butter in a frying pan and gently fry the onions. Add the honey and Genever and stir in. Season to taste with the salt and pepper.
2. Wash the meat, dab dry and trim off the bone. Season to taste with the salt and pepper. Heat the lard in another frying pan and fry the meat on all sides for approx. 5 minutes, then cut in half.
3. Distribute the meat cutlets in the raclette pans and cover with the onions. Sprinkle with the grated cheese and gratinate under the raclette grill for approx. 8 minutes.

Per serving: approx. 2 808 kj/668 kcal, 51 g P, 40 g F, 14 g C

INDEX OF RECIPES